# Classic Car
# Coloring Book

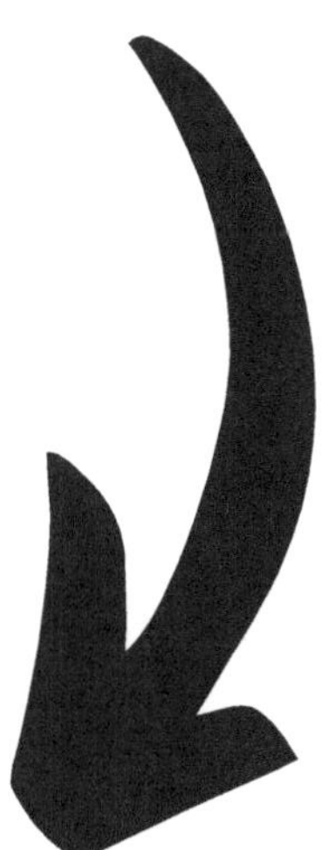

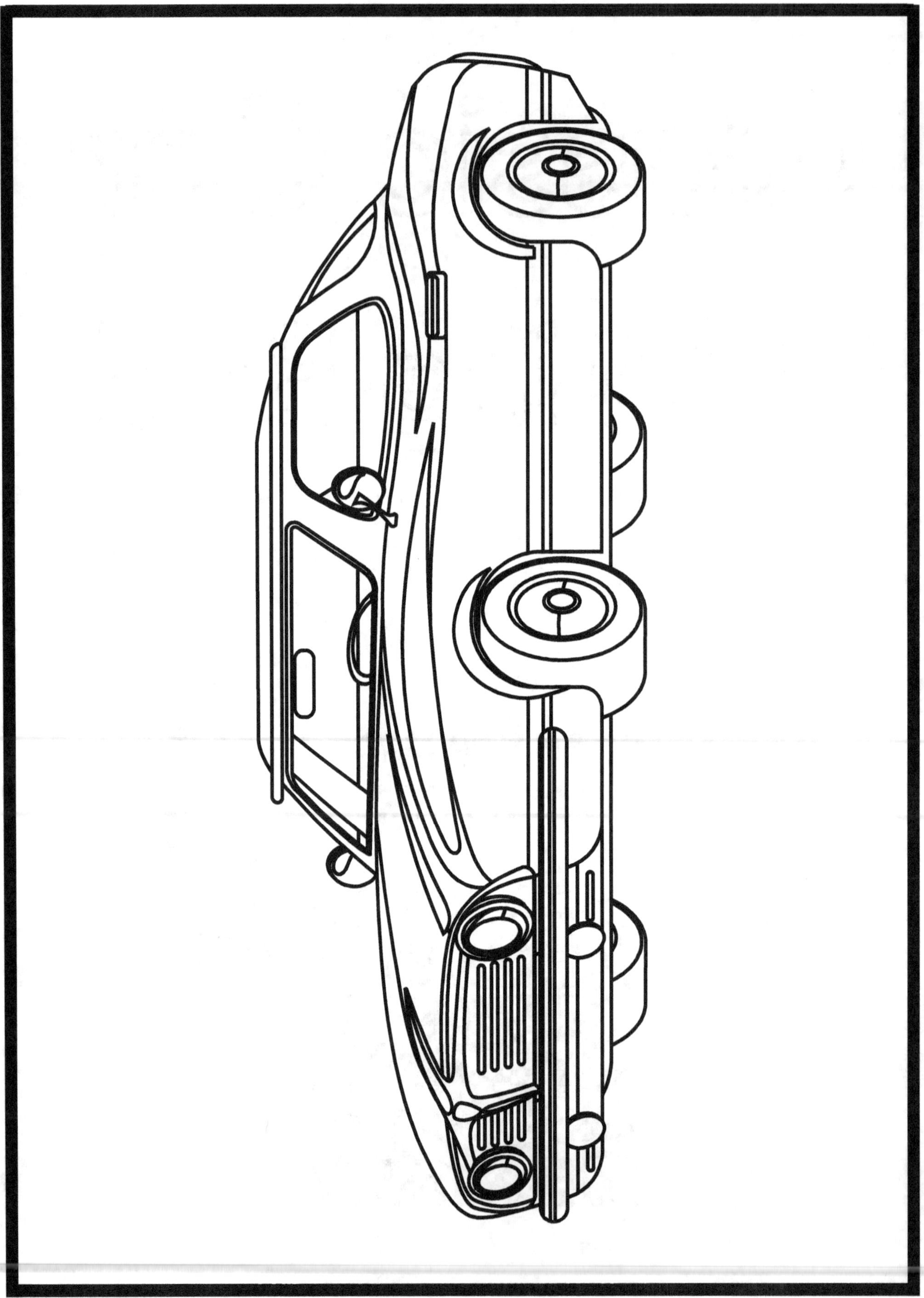

REPEAT

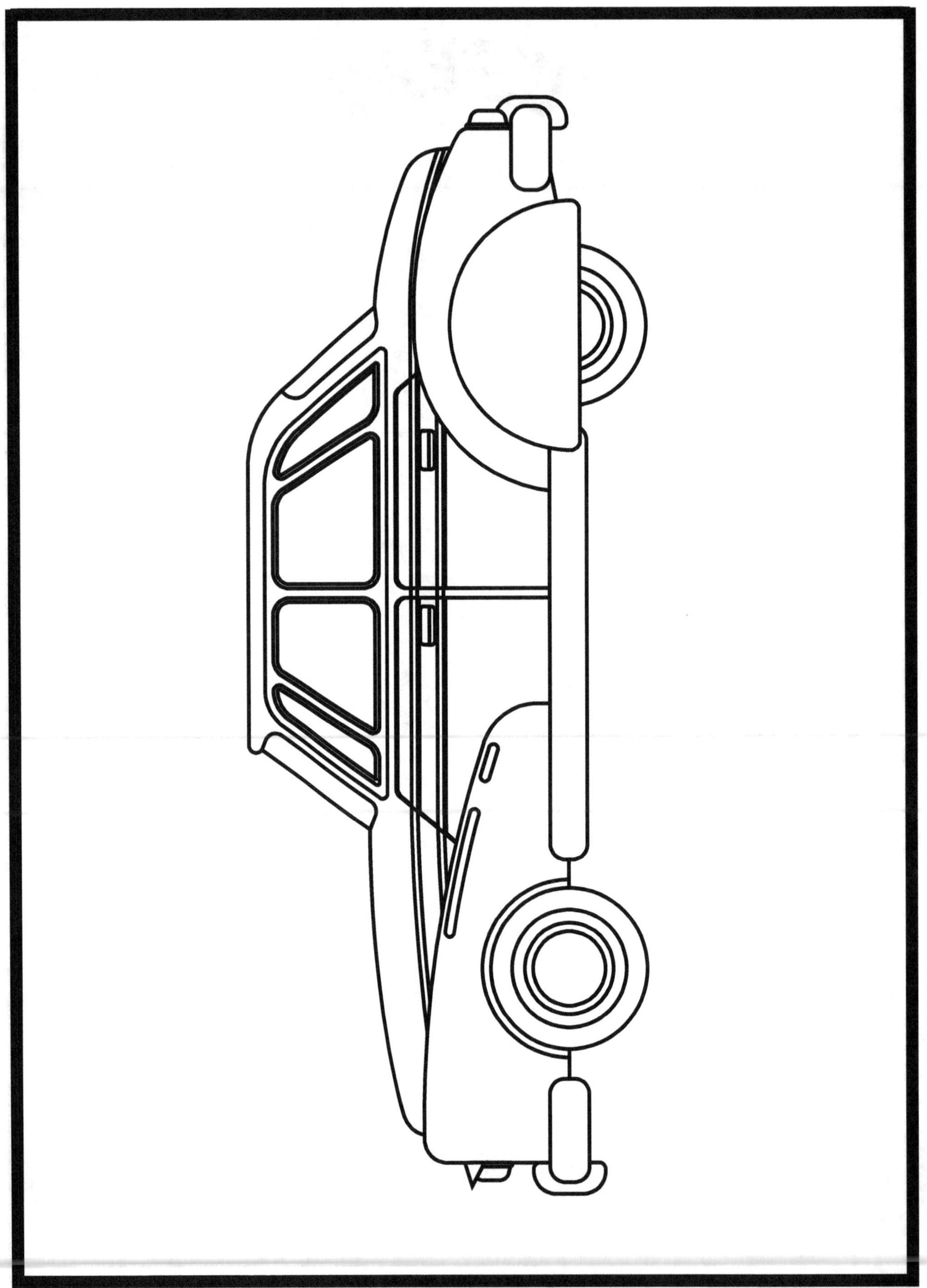

REPEAT

REPEAT

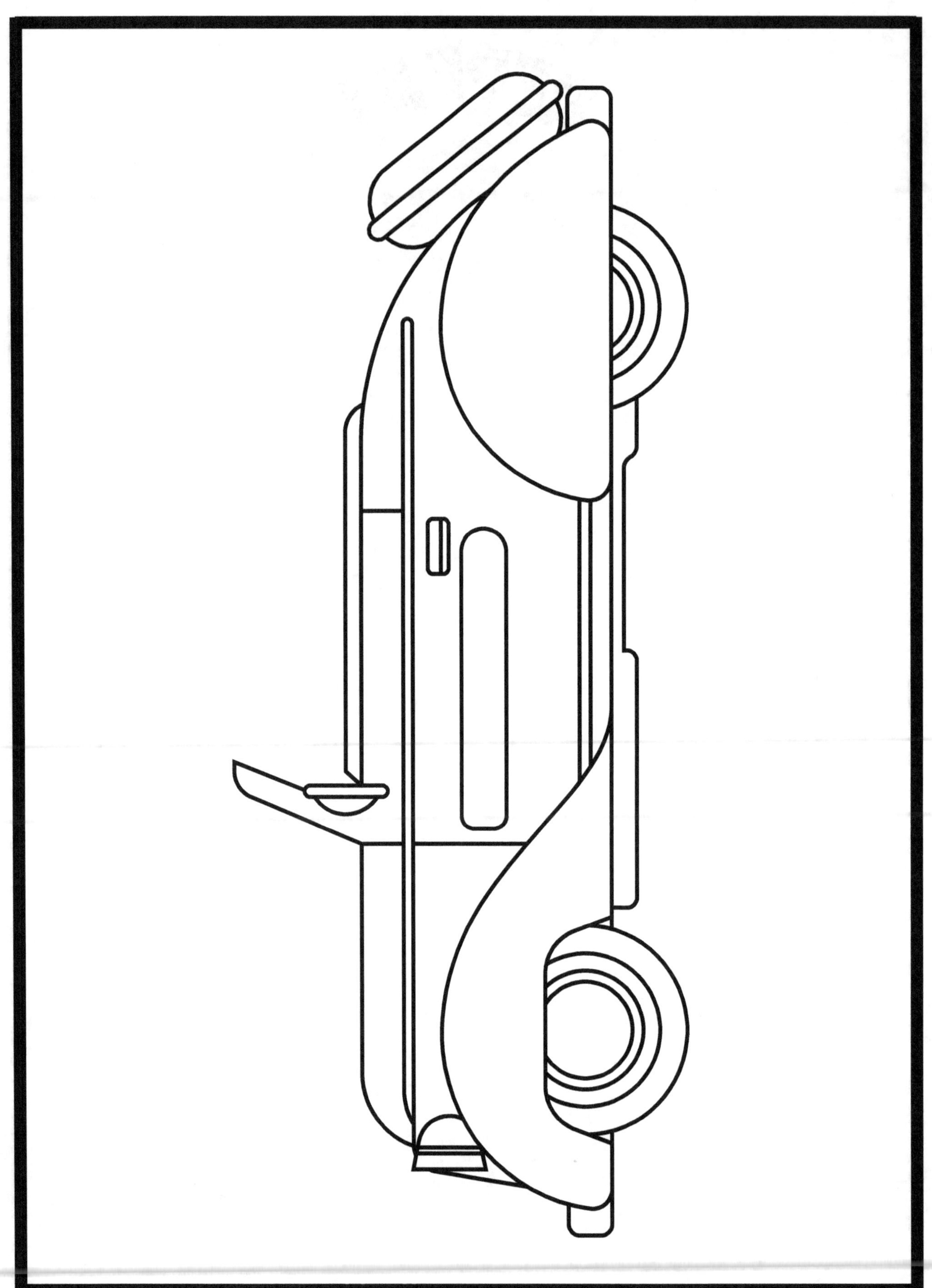

REPEAT

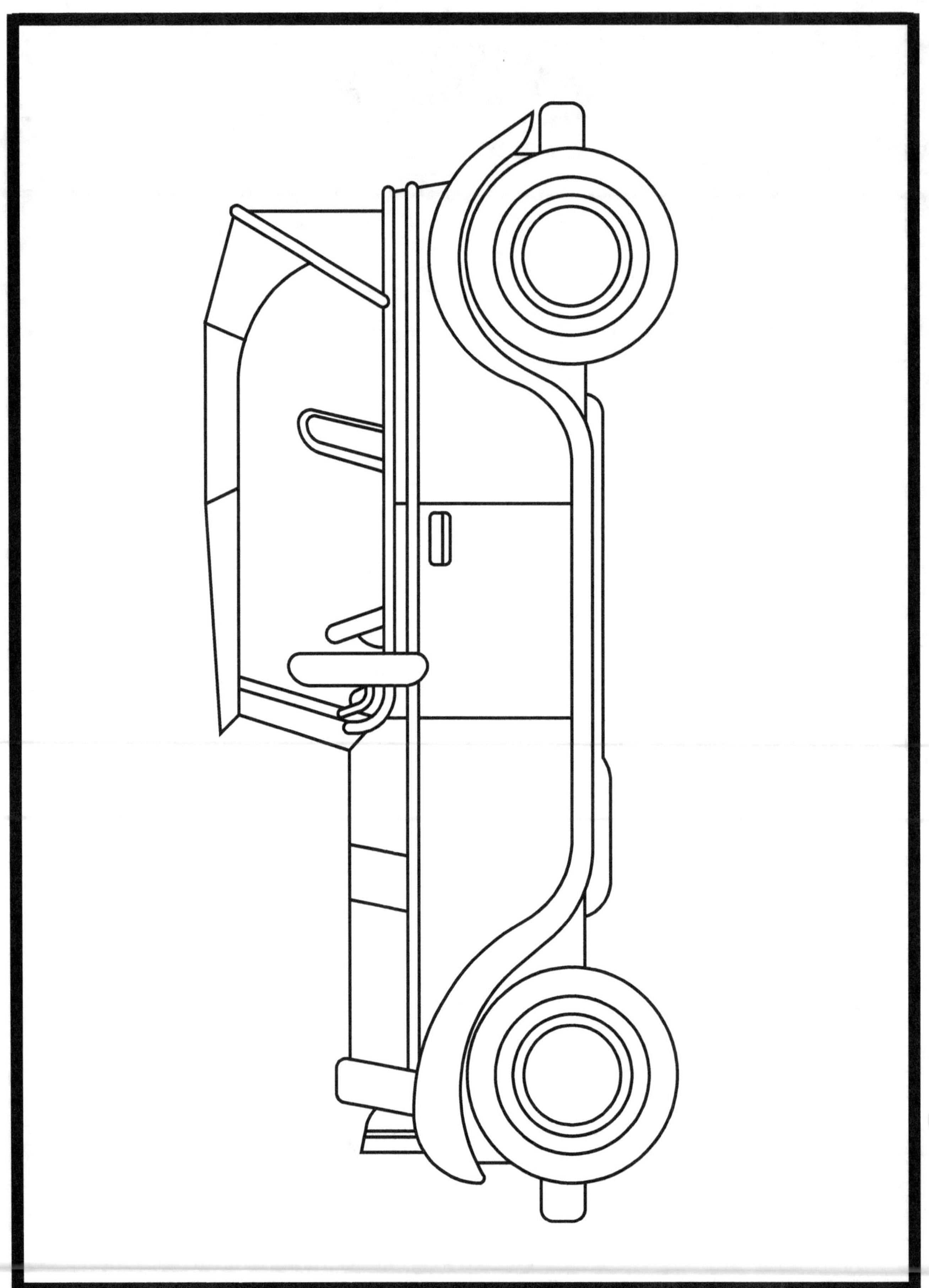

REPEAT

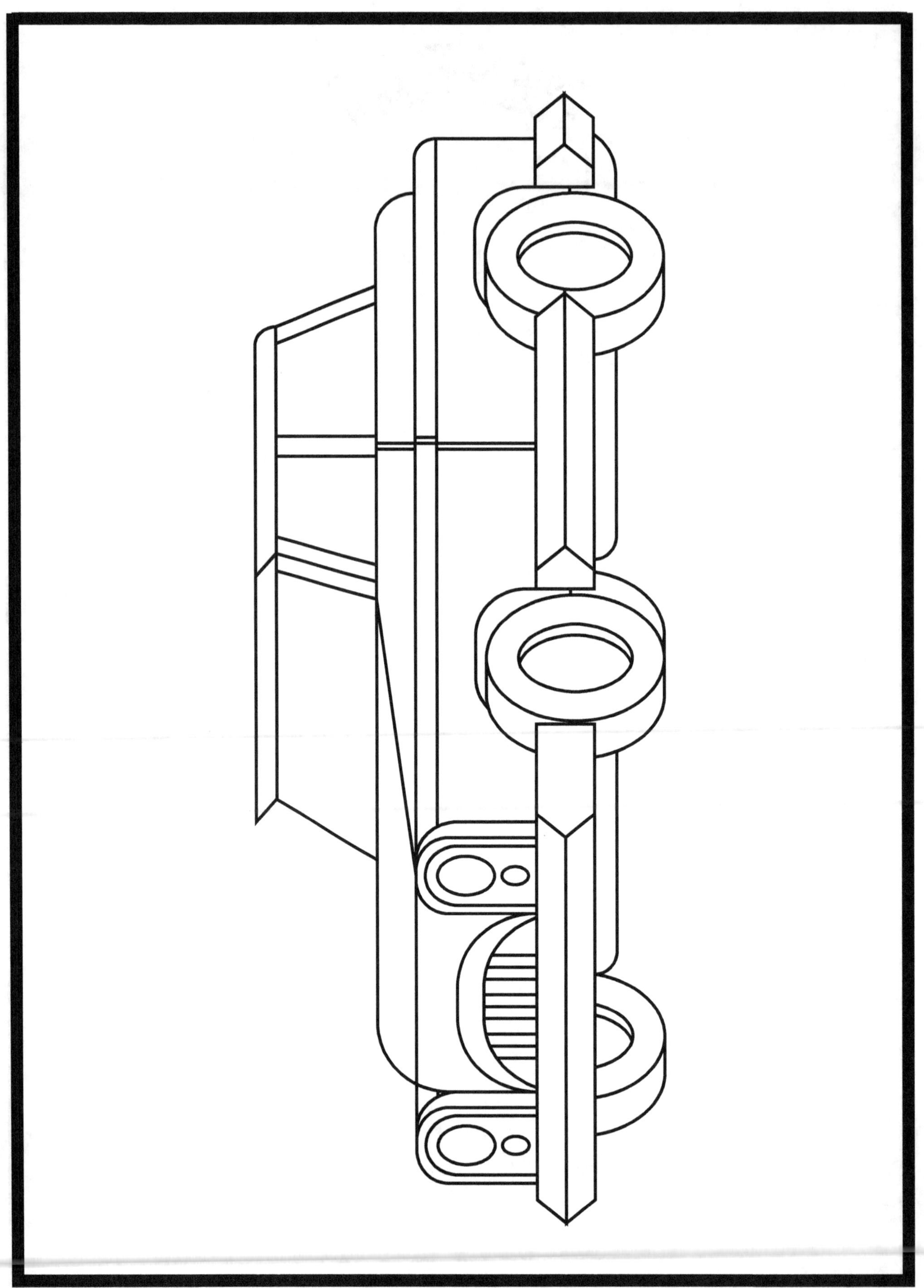

REPEAT

REPEAT

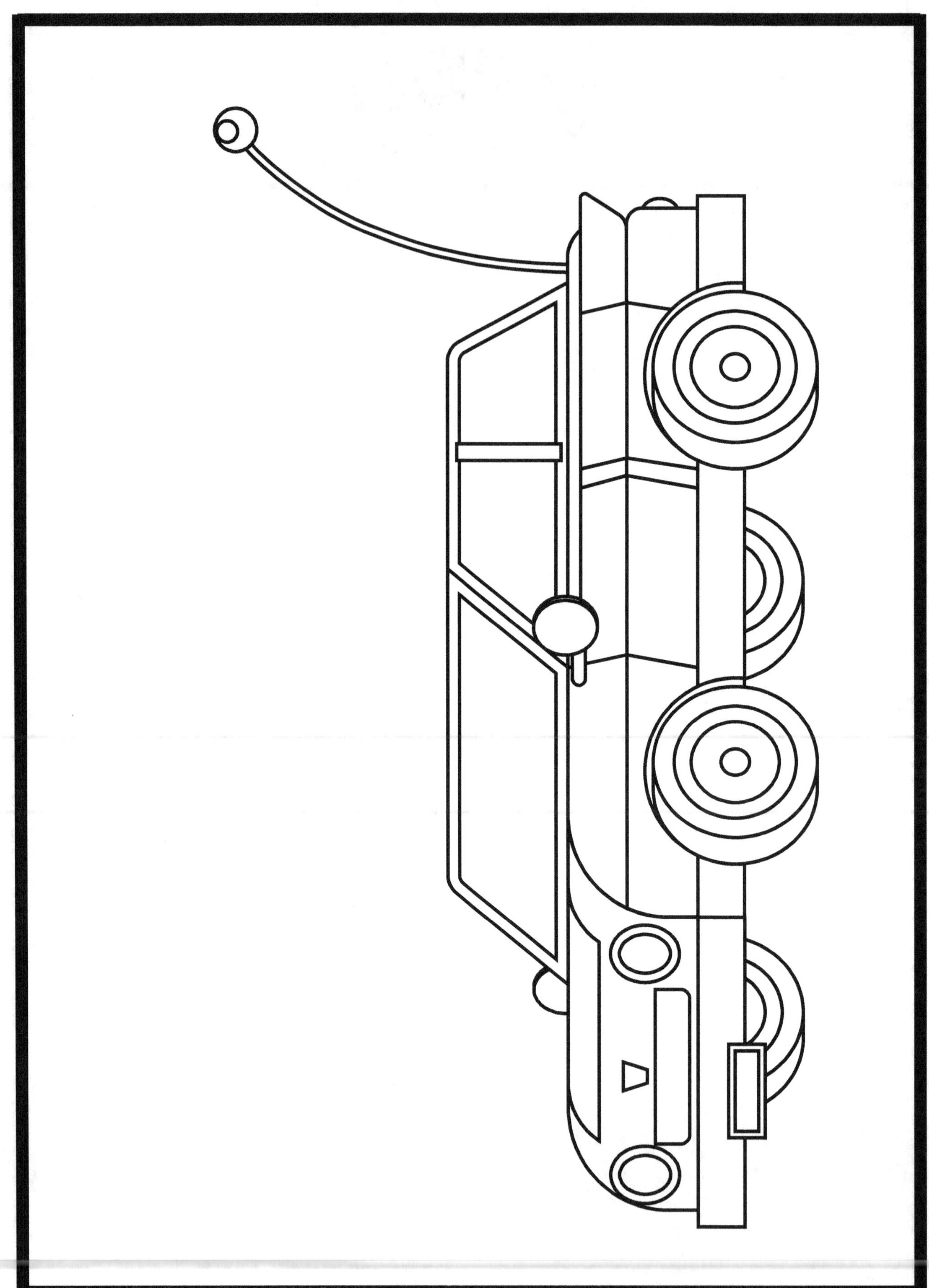

REPEAT

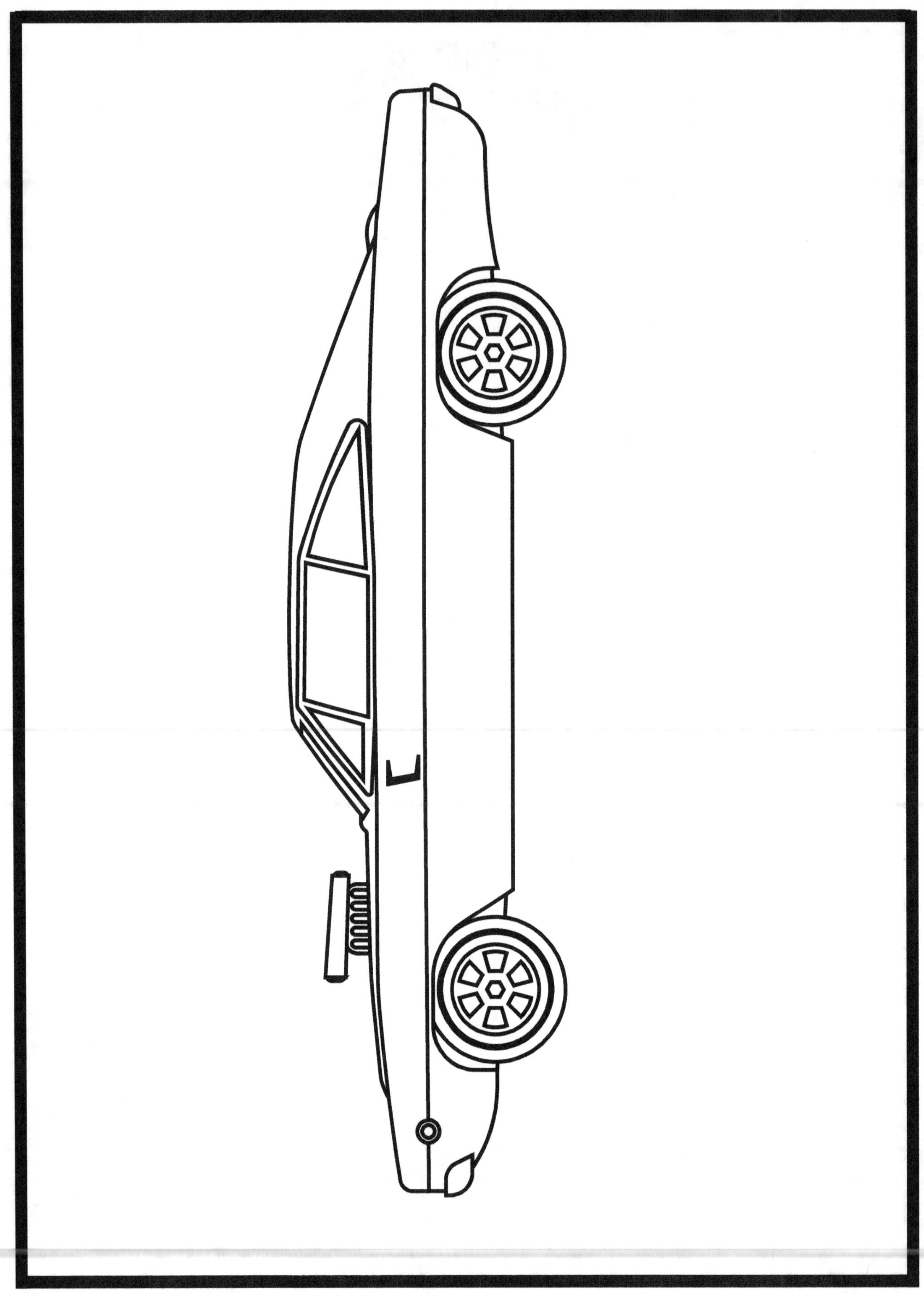

REPEAT

REPEAT

REPEAT

REPEAT

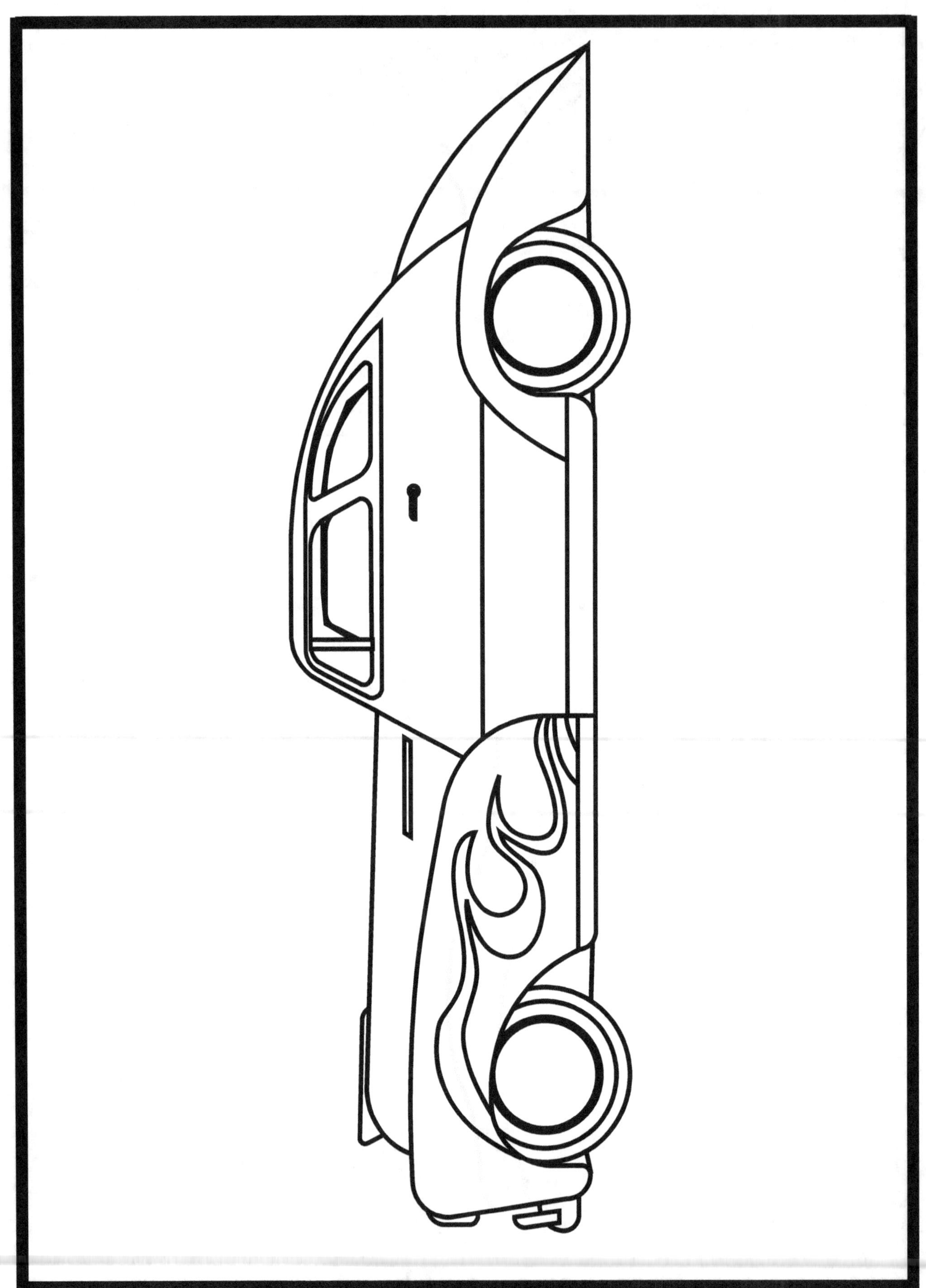

REPEAT

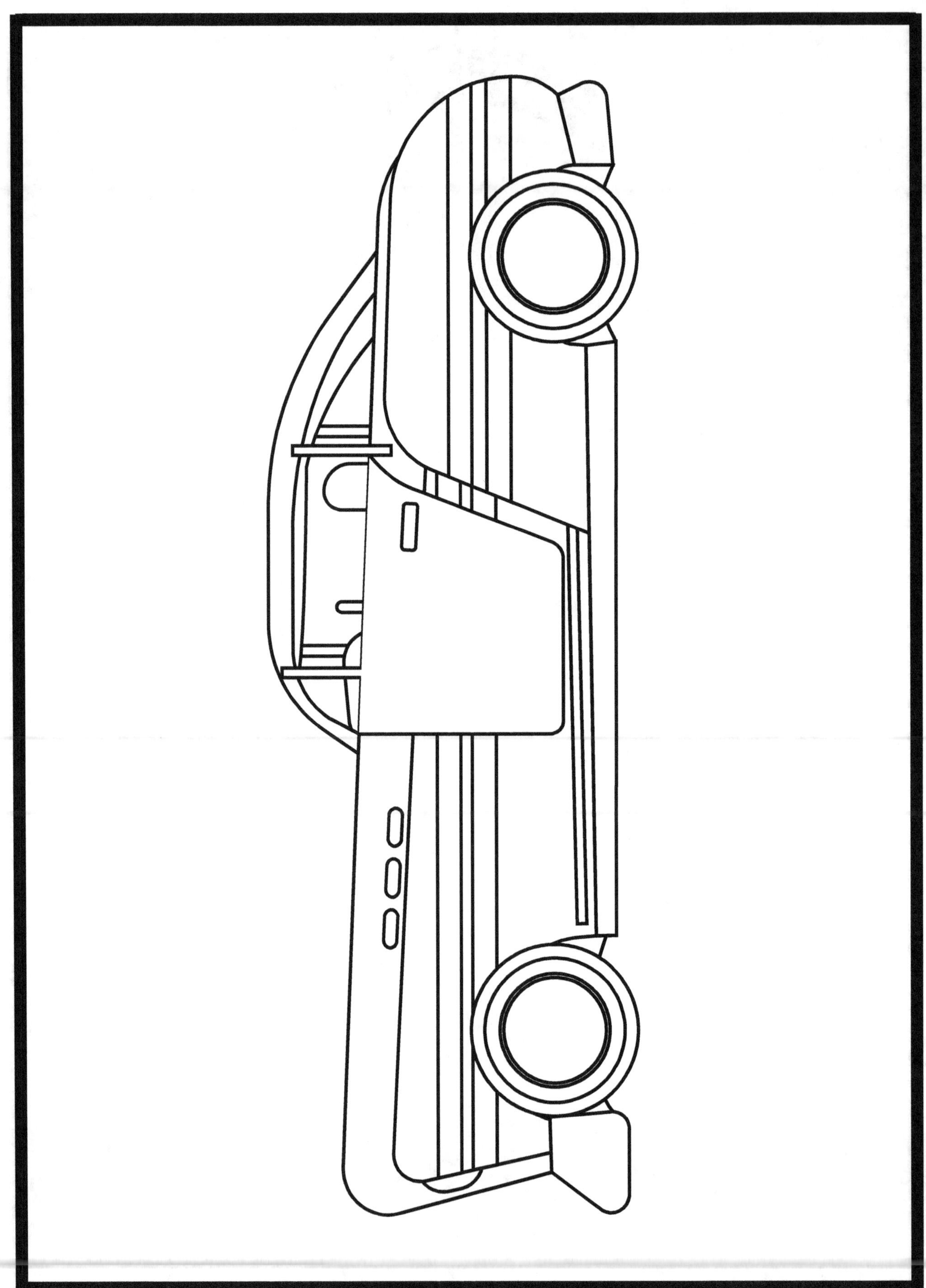

REPEAT

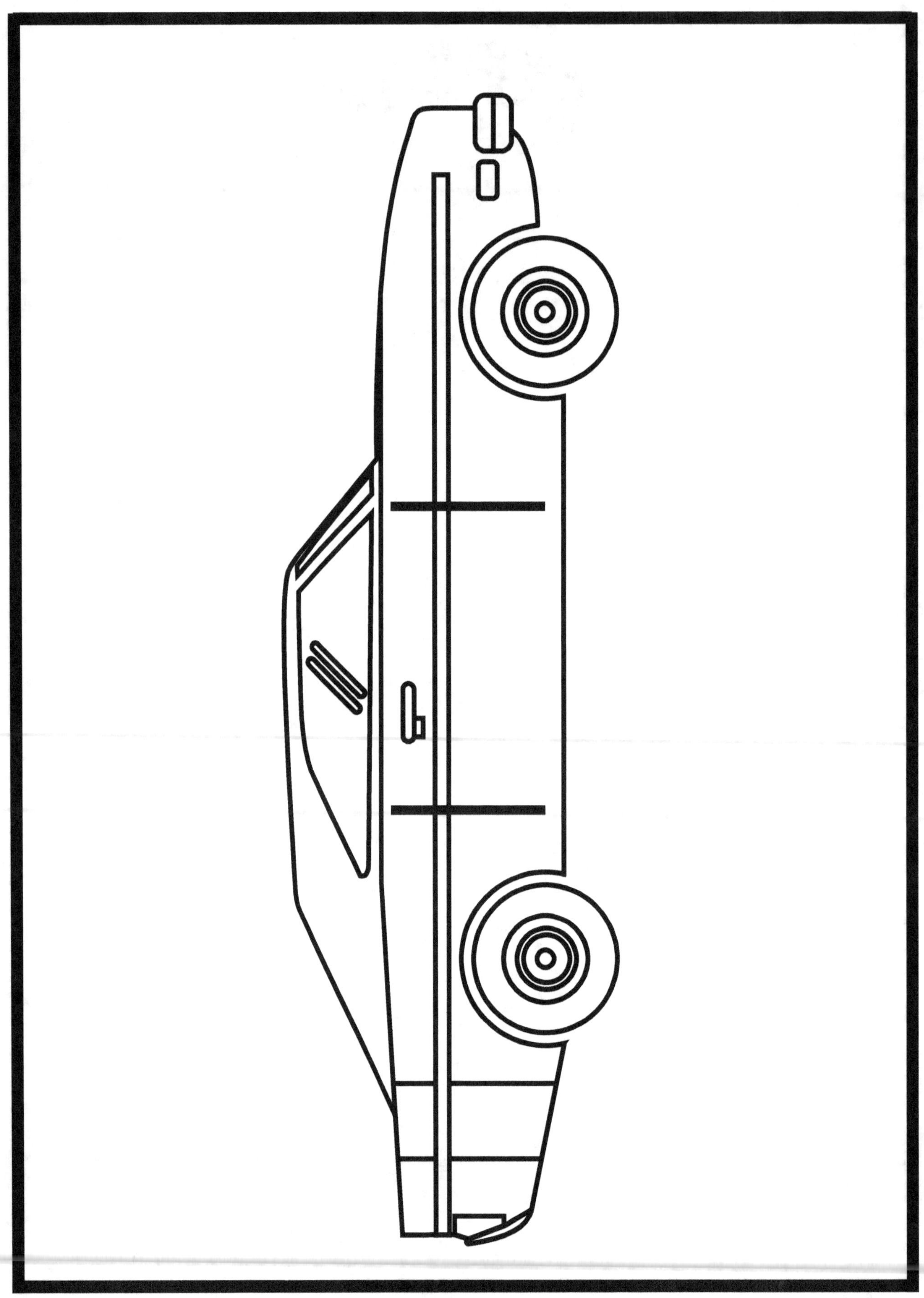

REPEAT

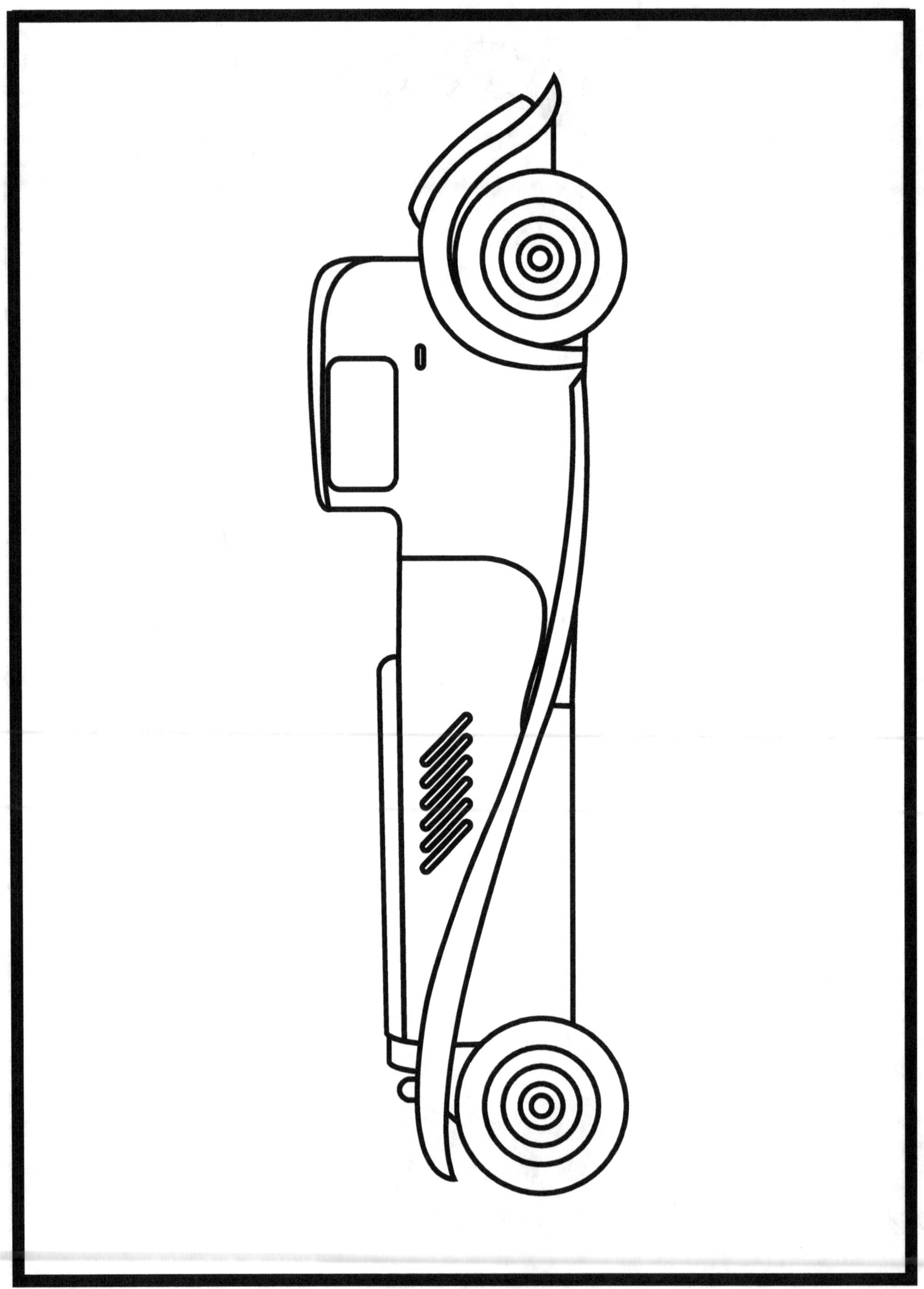

REPEAT

REPEAT

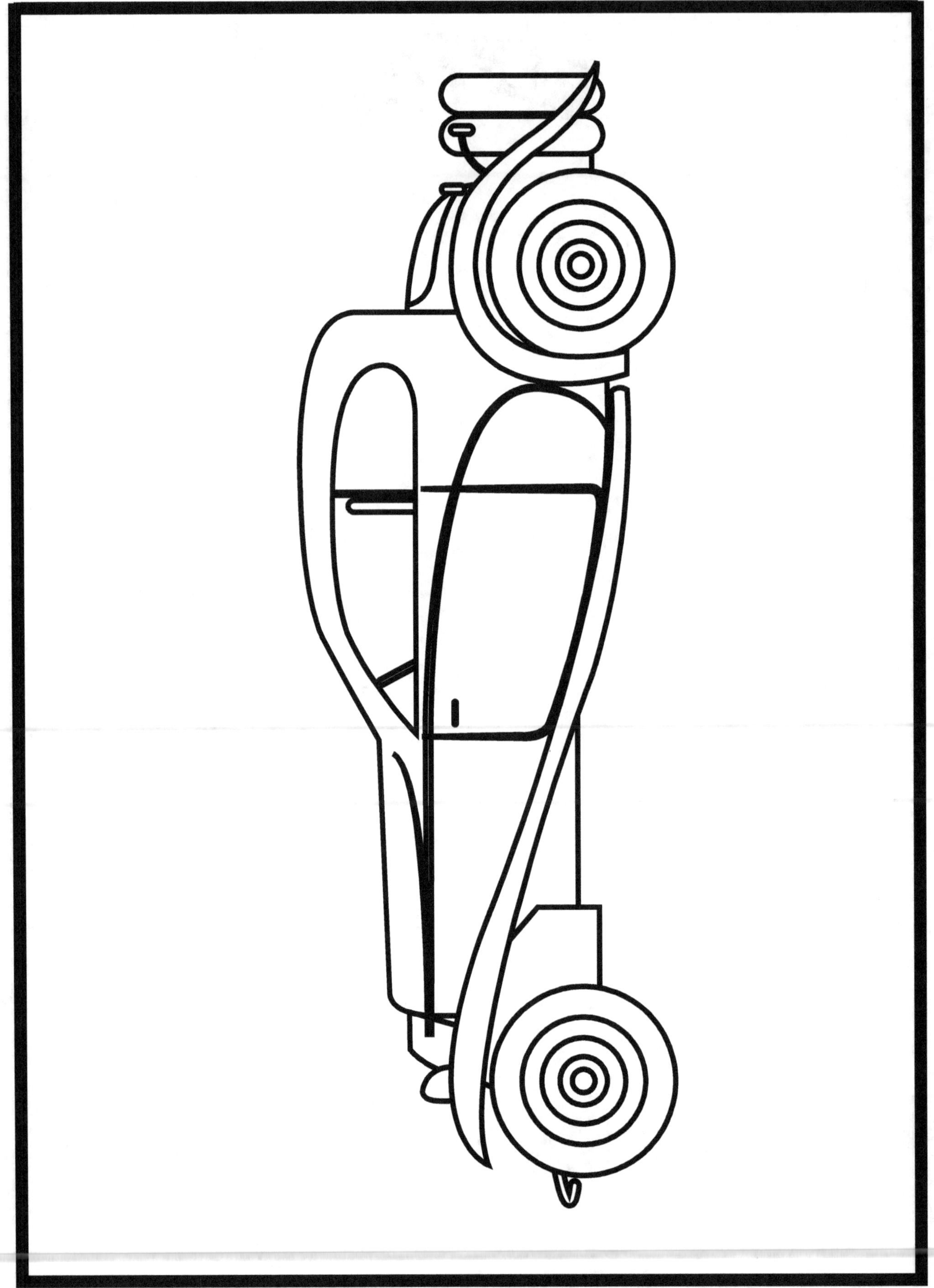

REPEAT

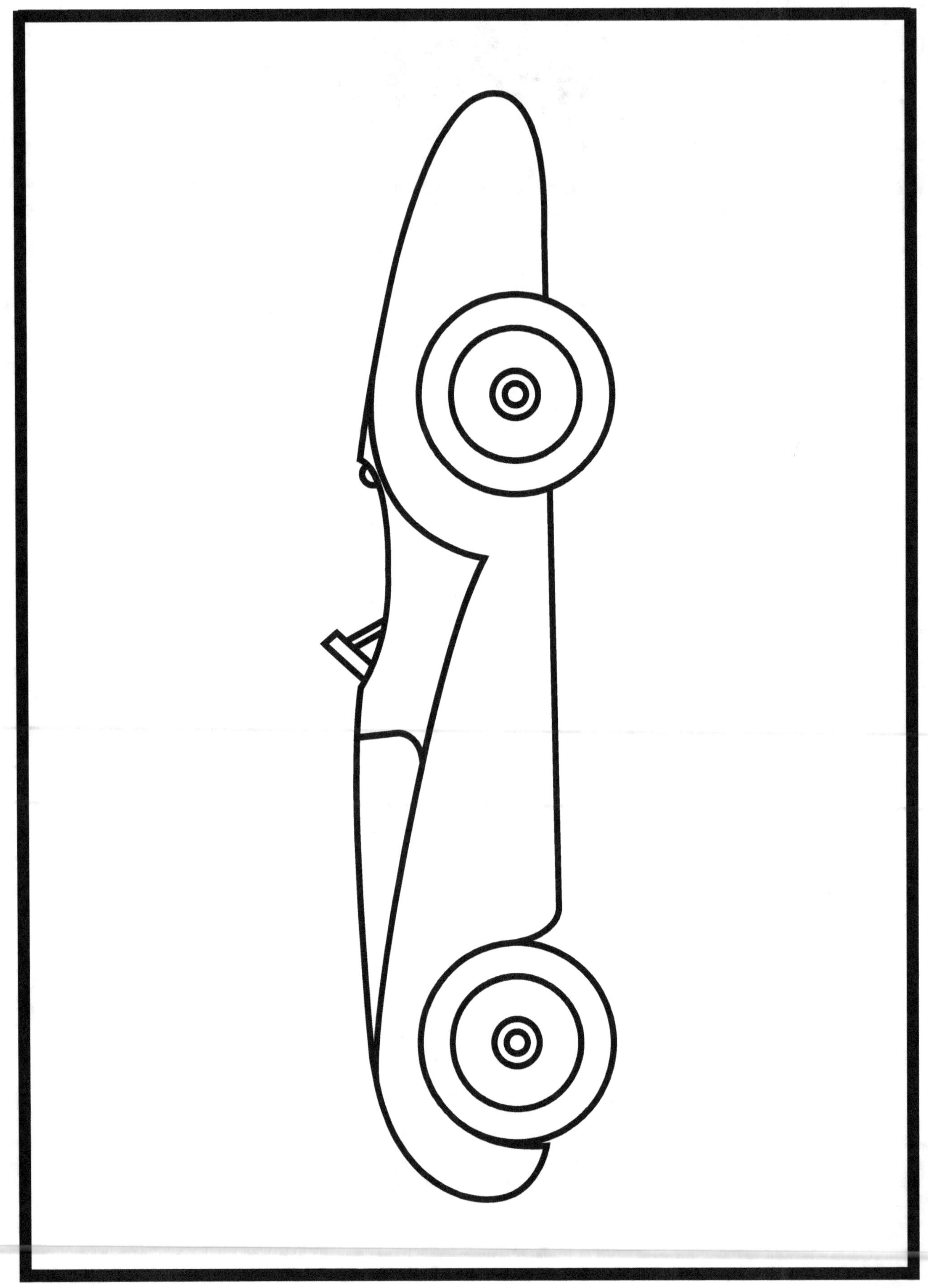

# REPEAT

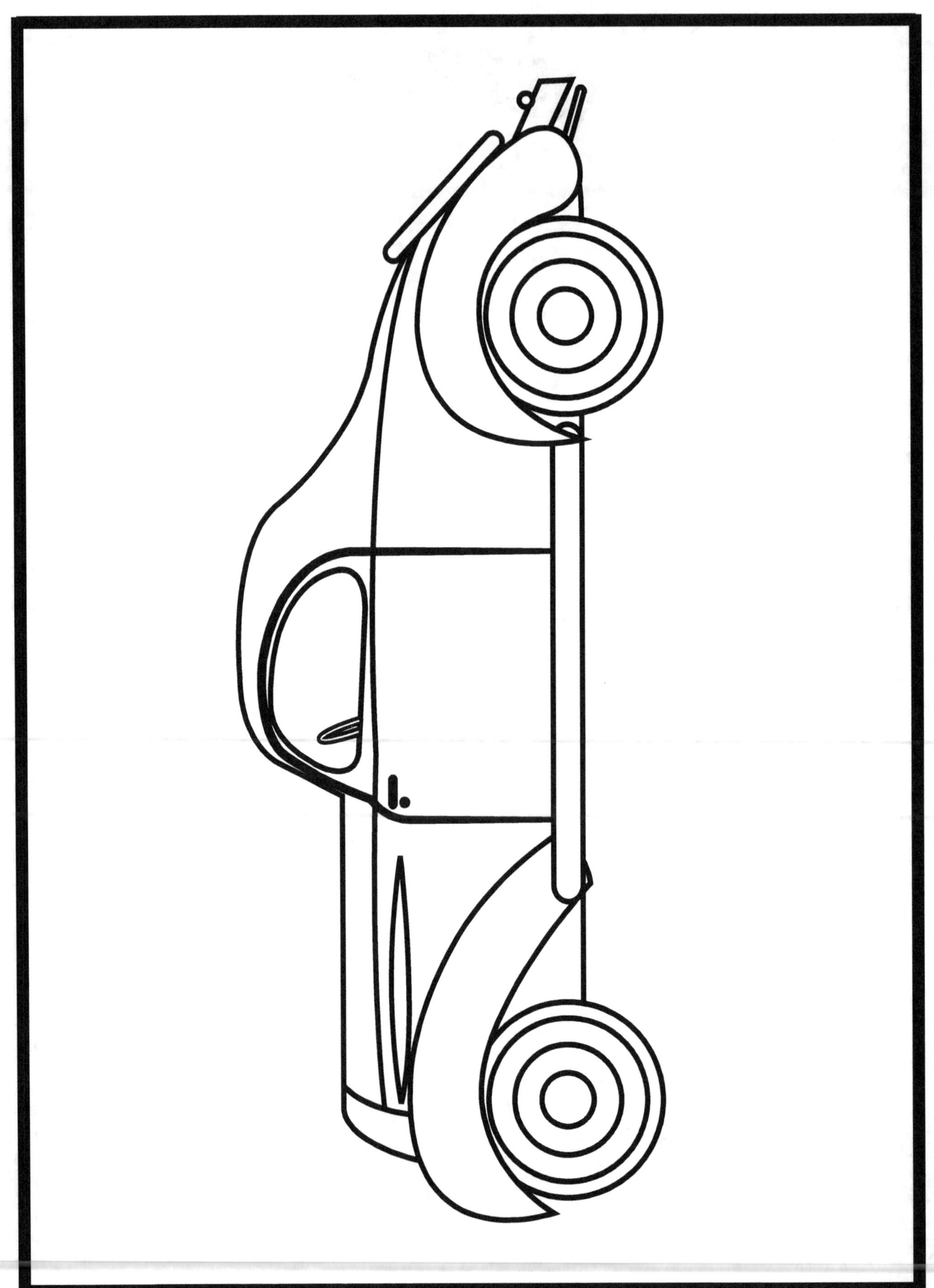

REPEAT

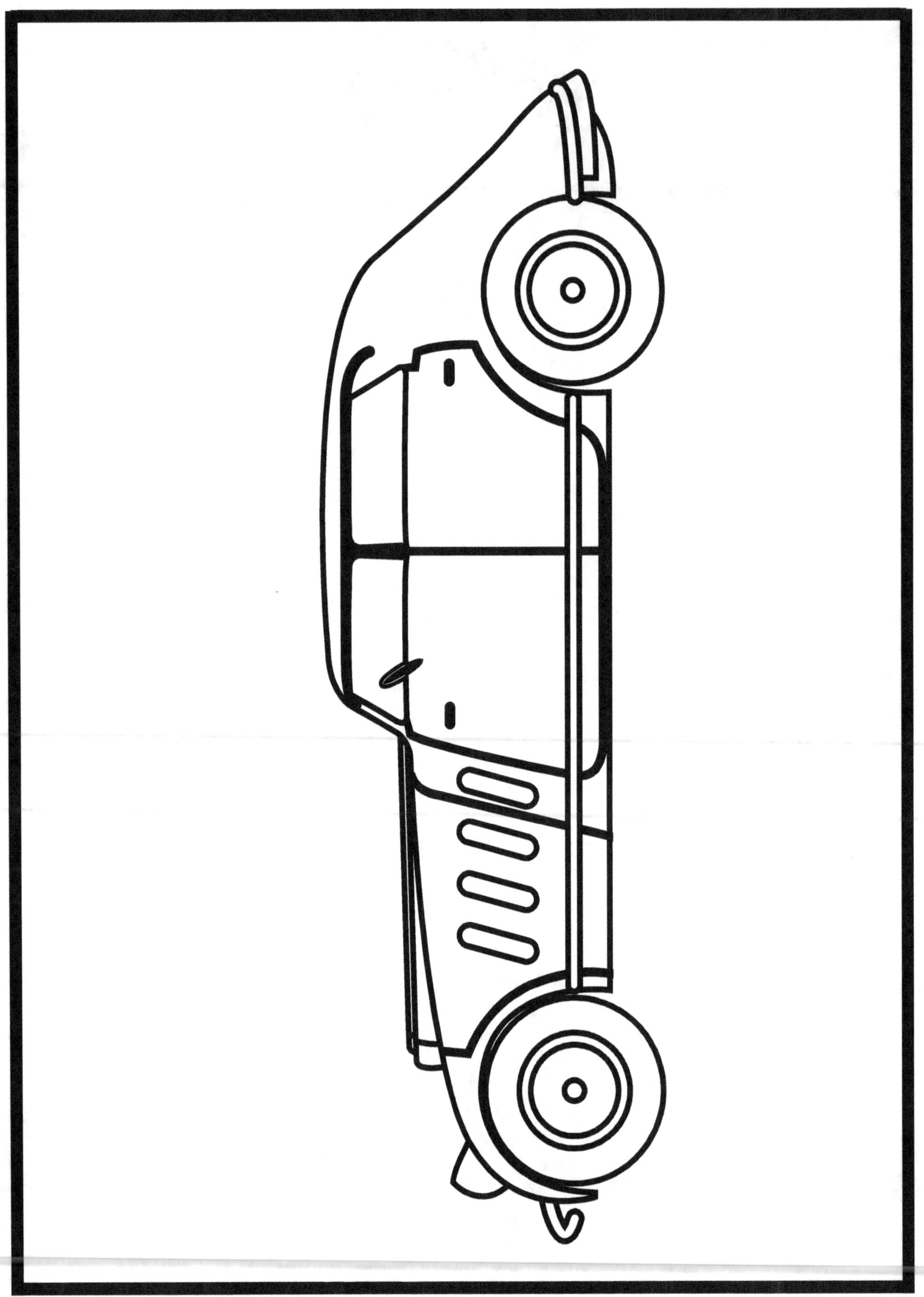

REPEAT

REPEAT

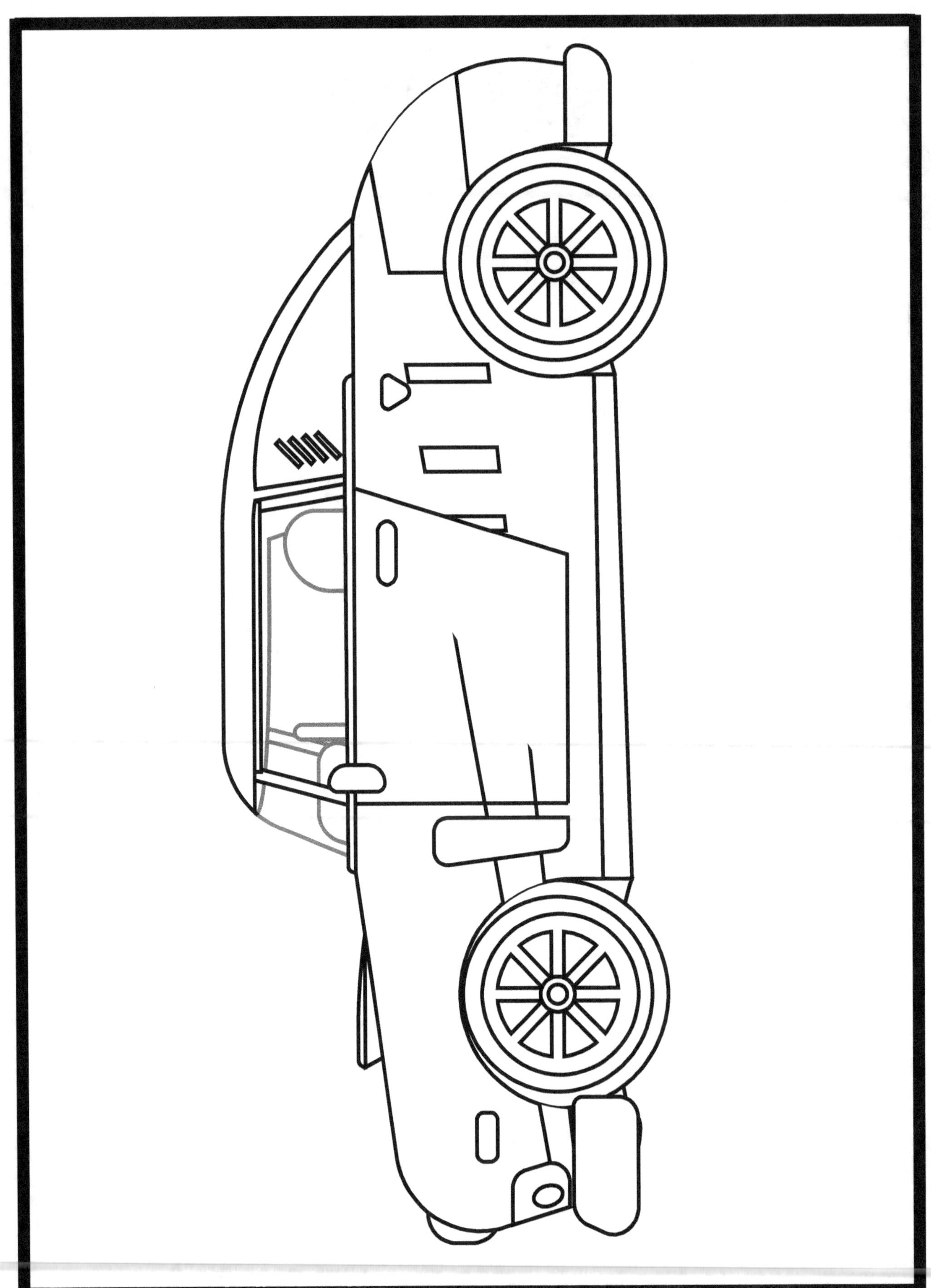

REPEAT

REPEAT

REPEAT

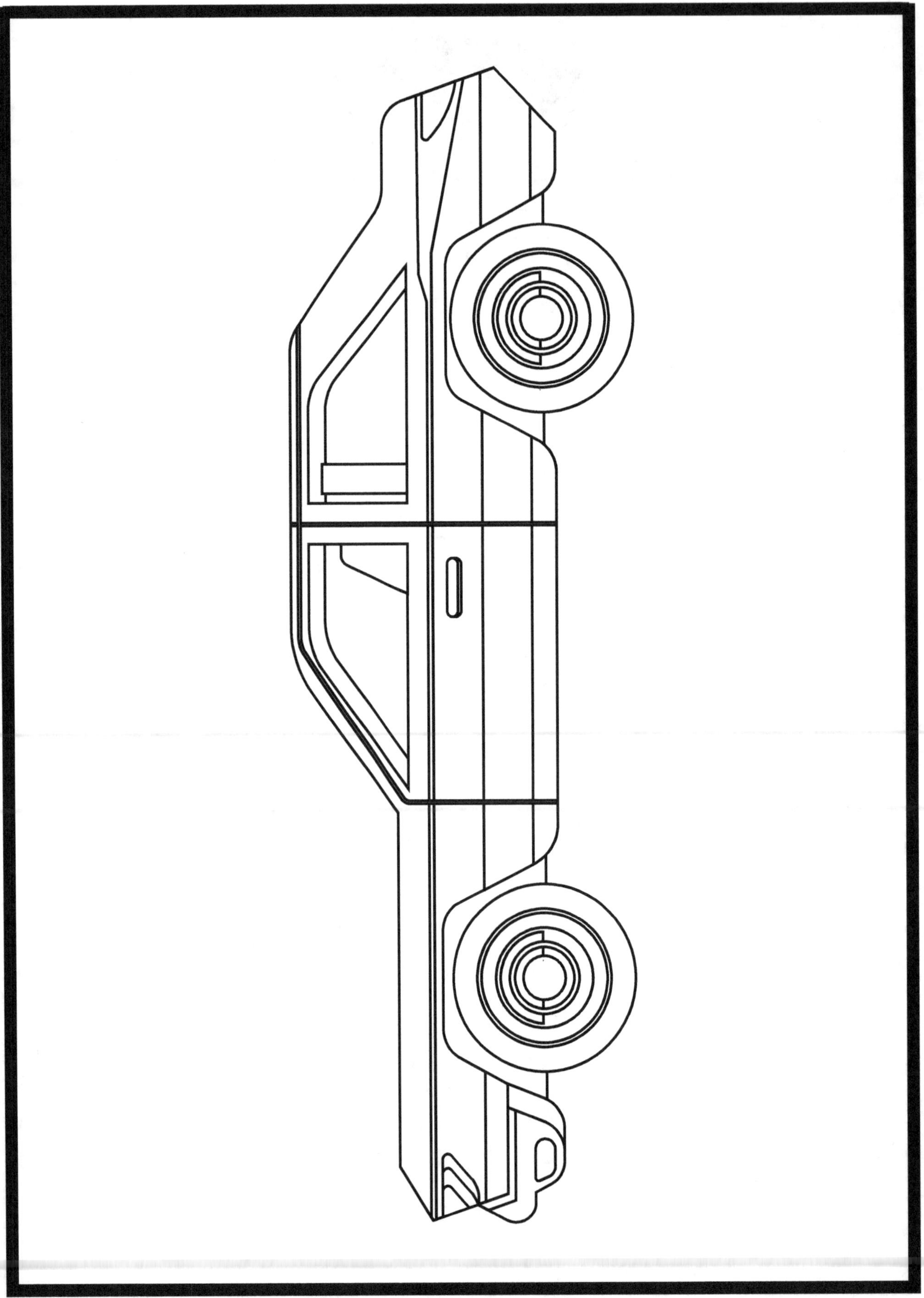

REPEAT

REPEAT

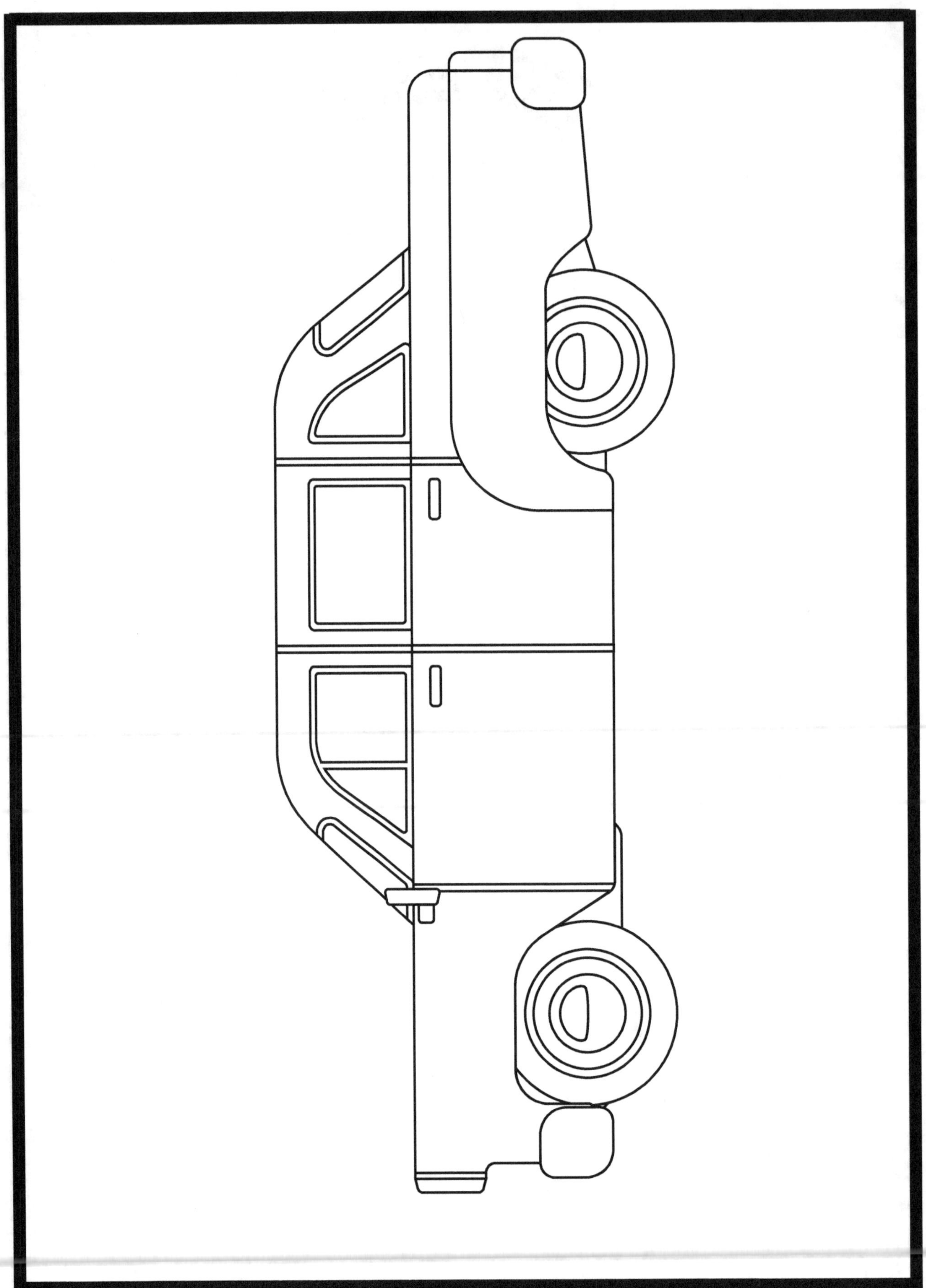

REPEAT

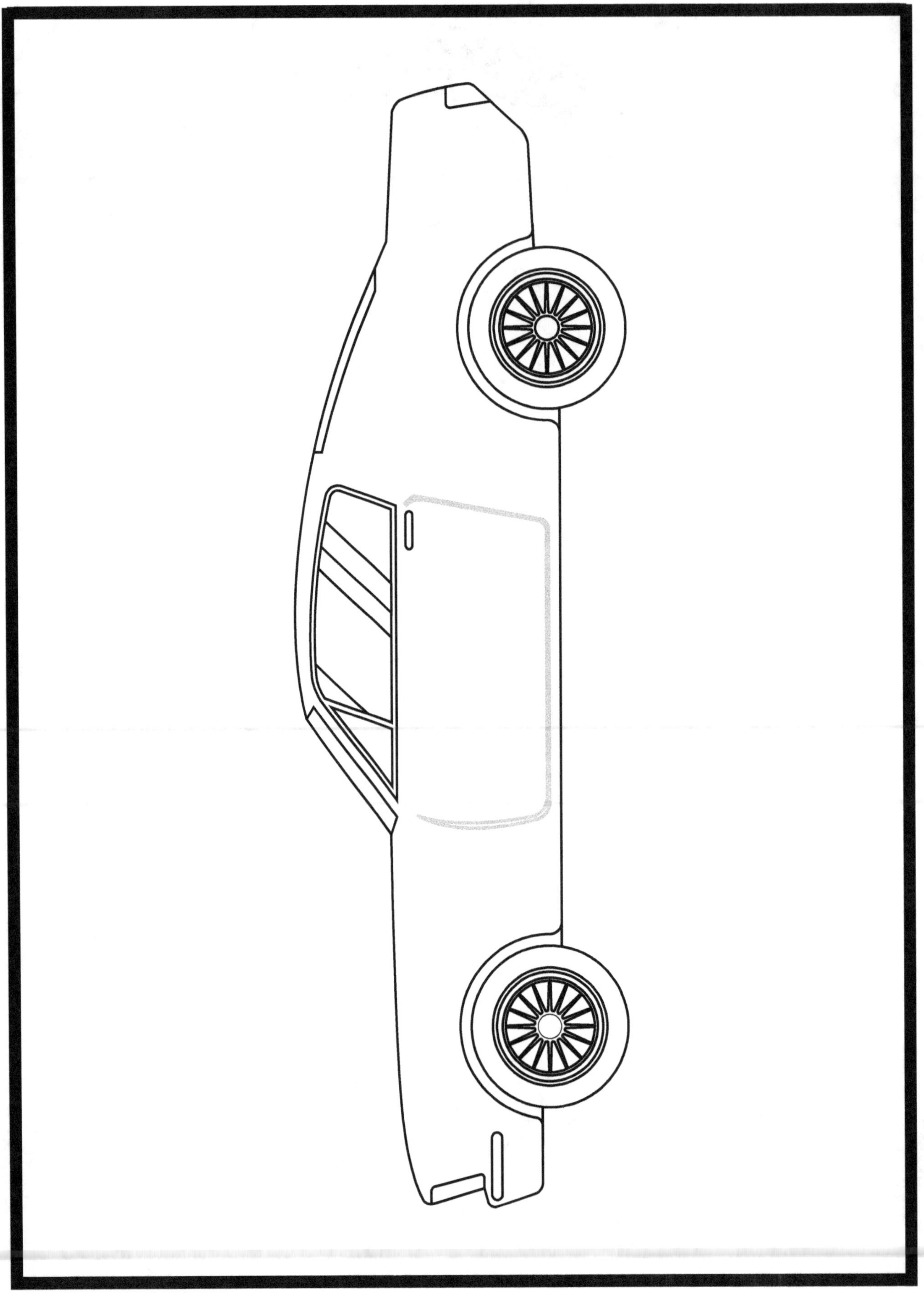

REPEAT

REPEAT

REPEAT

Our team has put a lot of work
into creating this book, we
would be grateful for sharing
your opinion about it.